Poems-for

Watanabe-Seitei

First published 2024 by The Hedgehog Poetry Press

Published in the UK by
The Hedgehog Poetry Press
5, Coppack House
Churchill Avenue
Clevedon
BS21 6QW

www.hedgehogpress.co.uk

ISBN: 978-1-916830-12-7

9 8 7 6 5 4 3 2 1

A CIP Catalogue record for this book is available from the British
Library.

Public Domain Artwork originally published in in the album "Seitei
Kacho Gafu" (1890–1891) by Watanabe Seitei, with thanks to RawPixel.

Contents:

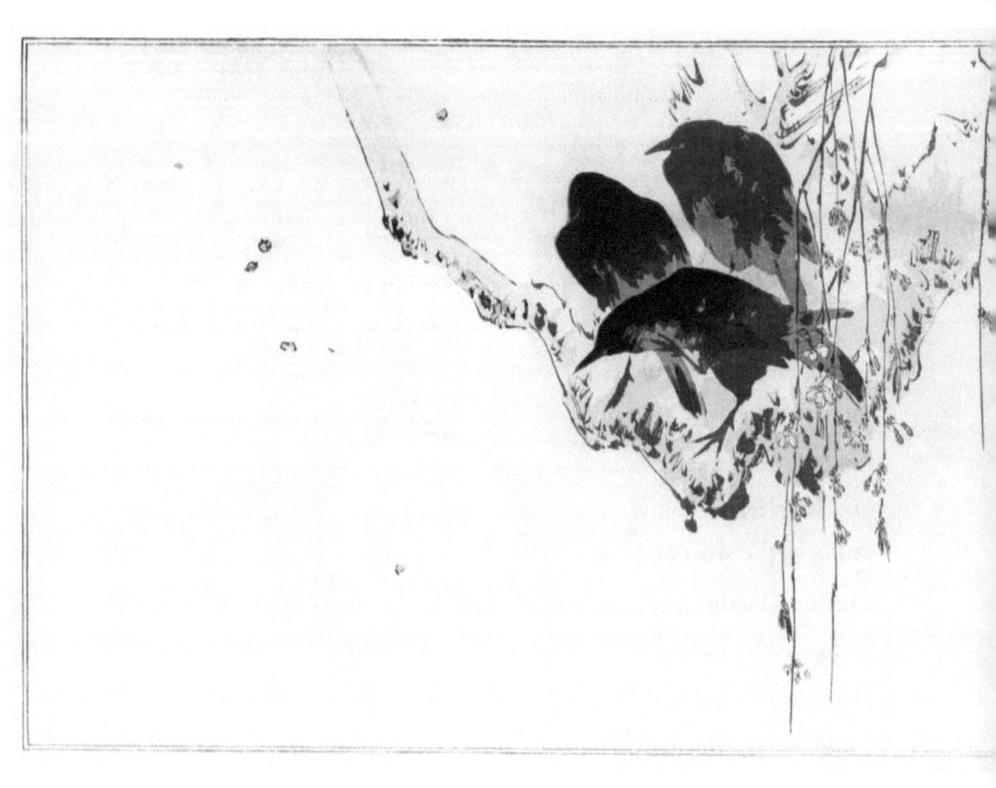

MARGARET ROYALL

On contemplating the work of Watanabe Shōtei

Simplicity enchants...
A single motif, a flower or bird
carefully placed on canvas

Sometimes an ensemble,
bird on bough, flower below
catching our attention

Pale wash or monotones,
camaieu of muted browns or greys,
a balm to soothe the soul

Sometimes a colour pop...
bright crimson or bold yellow
surprising the spectator

Calm, fresh perspectives
appealing in their tenderness
Nature's beauty extolled

Shōtei's Japanese background
distinguishable in each piece,
encouraging contemplation

RHIANNON LEWIS

A Watanabe Seitei Retrospective,

Compositions with flora and fowl.

Sepia-shaded scrolls,
Oozing inky lines,
Falling, like rain through trees,

Drop, composed,
Pooling into birds on branches-
Hunched, huddled crows,

Sparrows, perched, by
Blotched beech leaves,
Ducks hidden in rushes,

Egrets under a full moon;
Delicate lilacs, cascading,
Cherry blossom, bunched,

Placed, precisely;
Daubed detail swimming in
Watery, wistful washes,

Black base strokes,
Brushed into subtle colour-
Sage green, soft beige, deep rose-

Measured, elegant, refined;
A considered world, perfectly defined.

SHARRON GREEN

Shizukesa - Tranquillity

a haiku sonnet on the art of Watanabe Seitei

crow's 'Look at me' stare
draws fleeting gaze to drown in
orbs of wrinkled ink

willow tendrils swoop
leafy wistful lacy strokes
frame the waiting page

pale blossoms unfurl
gaily splayed sit pretty poised
fill the smiling eye

pools of pastel shades
blots of blushing beauty breathe
contrast with the void

nature nests in open space
artistry with poignant grace

NIGEL KENT

Dawning

marking Seitei's influence on Impressionism

A primordial pool
    of   ink
on silk
in which life
               stirs
evolves.

A solitary songbird that
       quickens
at his brush's touch
grows
      with
         each stroke,

    and settles
        on
an outstretched branch
of a yamakurze tree.

A bird that summons
         dawn,
its luminescence
         stretching
from   East   to   West

rousing
     weary artists
from their Montmartre beds

to see
        squalor washed
from their city's streets,
revealing the beauty
                hidden beneath

making Paris
            Paradise.

SARAH O'GRADY

In the gallery black

brushing West with East,
washi sighs, the cherry pressed,
ink-deep egrets wade,
goldfish flash then fade, misty,
the shishi-odoshi splash.

PATRICIA M OSBORNE

Watanabe's World

high in
maple's crown
crows squawk
          pecking
each other's ebony coats

flocks of magpies
          wock-a-wocking
                              dive
                              to
                              willow

          looking lost
          a duckling
          lowers
          his head
          nuzzles
     flaxen blooms

          a brimstone flutters around pine
rests its   buttery wings

          on a   windflower

pearly   petals   wave
          shielding a golden yolk

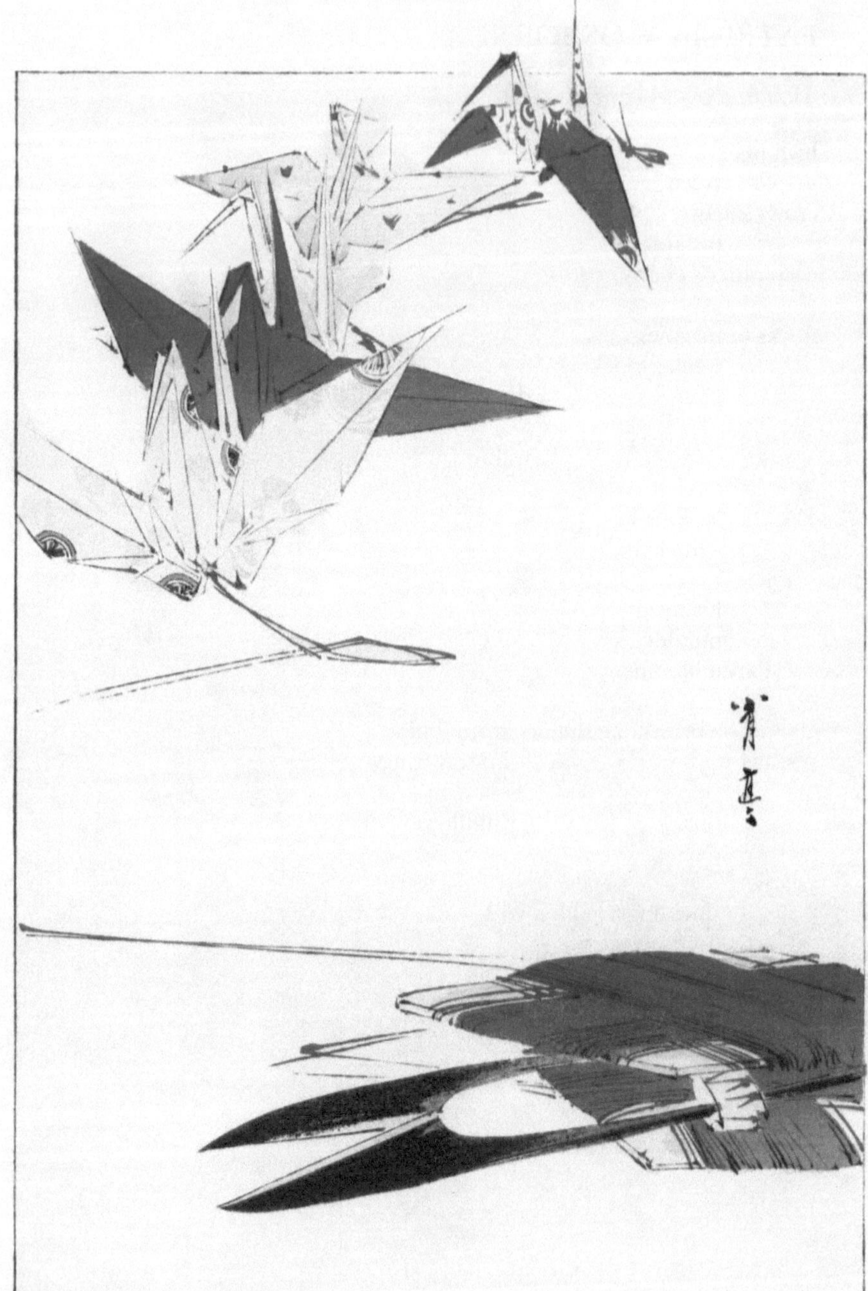

BRIAN MCMANUS

Feathered Friends?

Impertinent, Imperious, Impervious.
Demanding, Dismissive, Disdainful.
Unwilling, Uncaring, Unwavering.
As black as funeral silk, in a mirror
which casts no reflection.

Insentient, Inextirpable, Immortal.
Deliberate, Deceitful, Dominant.
Ubiquitous, Unethical. Unforgiving.
Life as a means to an end, in
a corpulent world of shadow.

No glint in the eye,
A cold, resonant, silence.
Icy winter stare.

CAROL LEE SAFFIOTI-HUGHES

In a Garden

I walk these paths in all seasons. Autumn brings the leaf fall, the must of earth dying into itself. Nothing so brilliant can stay. Winter garden with its silent, secret snow, its branches are brushstrokes. I follow mouse tracks, rabbits stark against white. Spring cherry blossoms drift to the ground, birds stirring for nesting. In Summer walks, heat rises,green beckons. But it is the time of year between them all that draws me. Liminal spaces. Stand between wind and rain, rain and snow, dark and light. It is then that dusk walks call.

> Three red berries, soon to drop
> Blue feathers rush to grey
> single bloom lingers against fading light

JOHN HERINGTON

Blackbirds

I really look forward to your daily visits.
Although we're separated by glass
you always turn me a glance before
chattering on.

You're motionless – I like that novelty –
you see no need to fly away quickly
while I always in lockdown mode
envy you the chance to wing it.

Why no sudden move?
Why no other place for you?

You're safe on your perch, that's it!
The topiary tree so high and close to me,
A Tree with a View – E M Forster knew
what an ivory tower could do!
no better place to view the world -
more worthy than grubbing below for worms
as most of us do.

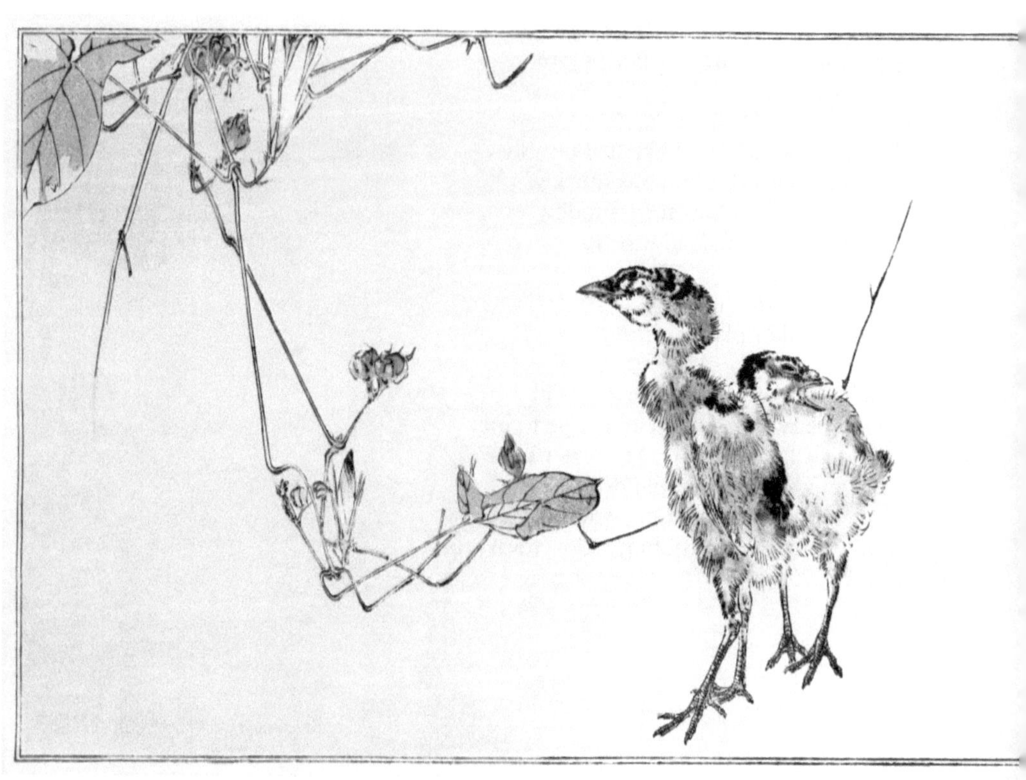

ISABEL MILES

Space

Here, art makes visible the empty distances
that are the greater part of everything,
from atoms up to galaxies.
Space is as necessary to birds as wings
as central to electrons as their spin.

Poised in a perfect equilibrium,
the stillness of what is
is caught and held in light, motionless,
yet quick with latent movement.

These seeming-solid birds,
flowers, butterflies and branches,
mostly space themselves,
splash dark against the empty-seeming air.
But nothing here is black and white.

OZ HARDWICK

White, Interrupted

Thin twigs finger distinctions –
sky/pond/paper – and the year rinses
out its ochre glow.

Birds are old souls, huddling for
warmth and gossip, sharing smoke until
they themselves are clouds   dispersing.

We know all the angles of this small
world – we were young/lost/awake but
dreaming – and we know each smudged
skeleton leaf, each sharp beak calling
here here here.

Every touch is a soft brushstroke. Every
bird – light/flutter/absence – is a year
folding itself away.

Every glimpse, every thought, is as
precise as cracked ice.

CEINWEN E CARIAD HAYDON

Haiku for Watanabe Seitei

your soft inked brush
integrates the separate
with crystal clear lines

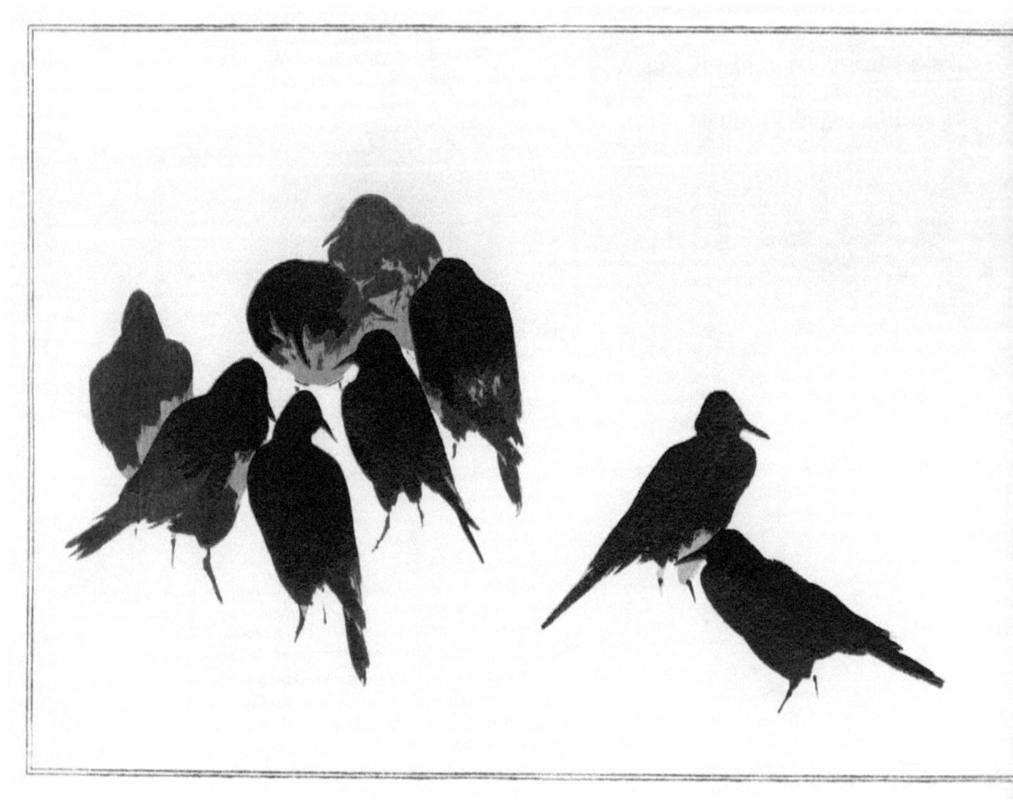

CHRISTINE TOKUNAGA

Flight

black hair
in the wind
the small girls
turn in circles

five small girls
extend their arms
their black hair
how it flies

black hair flies
in the wind
the five girls
turn in circles
white skirts
swirling

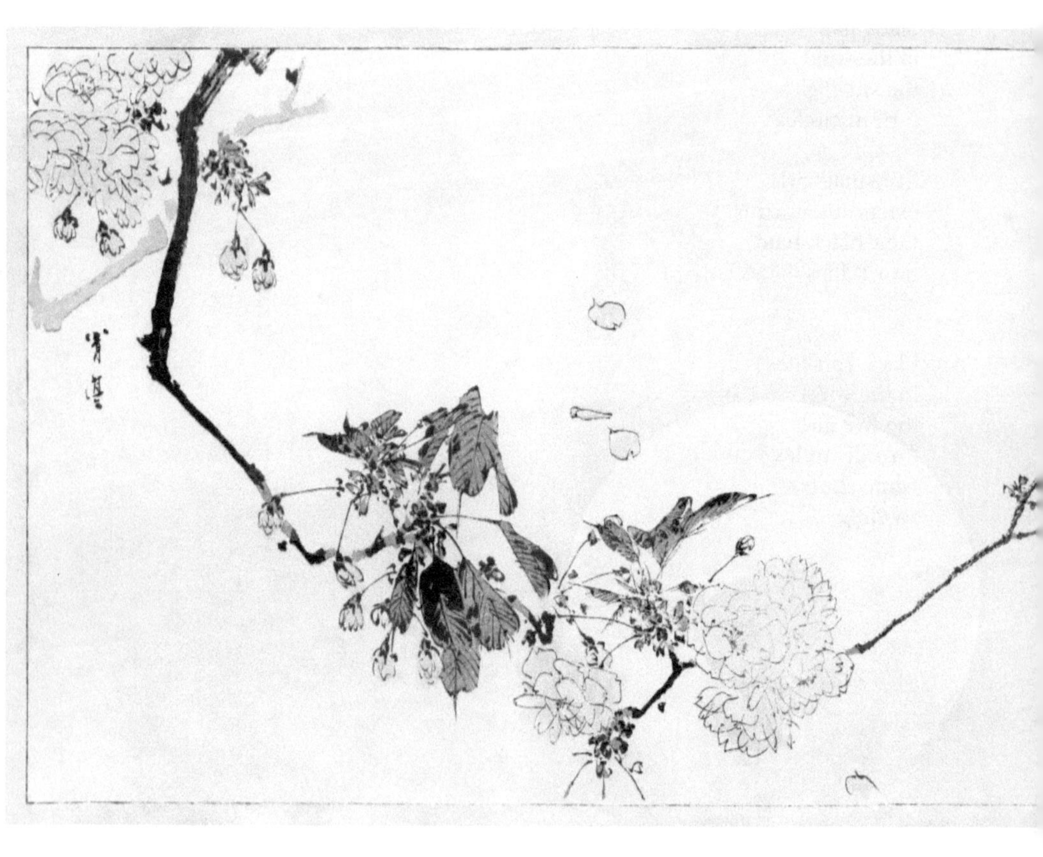

SASKIA ASHBY

Love will even reach the crows on the roof

The warmth of your heart infuses moss with green,
    liquifies resin to heal bark, breathes flight to ladybirds.

The warmth of your breath incubates larks eggs, unfurls fern croziers,
    uplifts sycamore seeds.

The warmth of your hand cradles pinecones, coaxes salamanders,
    draws up spring water.

The warmth of your gaze brings blush to foxgloves,
    ripens blackberries, convexes hazelnuts.

The warmth of your skin is a den to earth in, a honeycomb melting,
    a cloud dissolving.

The warmth brings swallows, magpies, ducklings,
    seagulls, crows and cranes.

Flocks of birds fly from fourteen thousand islands to perch on your roof.

HAZEL STARRITT

Exile

A breeze slips in through the open window,
the woman barely stirs in response to the intrusion.
A partially worked embroidery cloth lies idle in her lap,
Black silk thread trailing from a tiny needle.

Once she was a woman of some importance,
Enjoyed the status due to the wife of a powerful man,
With his downfall and demise, her world collapsed,
Now she is nobody, her very existence forgotten.

She sighs heavily into the enveloping silence
Her hands move to resume her embroidery
The rhythmic stitches that ease the headache
and fill the lonely minutes and hours.

The image she creates with her black silk thread,
reflects her mood, echoes the hollowness within.
Sparse leaves adorn the fabric on solitary branches,
Black on white, no colour to give warmth or richness.

It drew her in, this scratched image, half-erased.
A meagre monochrome, on limp scrap of fabric.
In it she sees herself, an ethereal shadow,
confined within a colourless, grudging existence,

Once her life was like a richly woven tapestry,
full of life and colour and constant noise.
So many people surrounded her at court,
women vie-ing for her attention, men for her favours.

She shudders remembering the constant whispering,
The fierce eyes of enemies glinting in the dark.
A flame of anger surges within - her needle stabs.
A tiny crimson drop trembles, and falls onto her lap.

Lowering her gaze, she surrenders herself to her stitching
the quiet repetitive motion restoring calm.
Now, a blood-red flower unfurls its petals beside her needle
and, for a while, displaces the spectre of the past.

GRETA ROSS

Worm lines

birds as linocuts
in the cold dawn on branches
silvered in the haar

scattered leaves stir
hunched in mist a cat eyes
busy robins scrabble

ghost-like skeins of ice
worm lines knitting the wet soil
white trails glistening

JACKIE TRUMAN

Crow

The birds gathered, crows, black ominous, a murder. They stood, a collection of ebony-feathered warnings like mourners at a funeral. He, watching through the window, collected ink block, soft brushes and water. The brushes, bamboo handles held straight in their pot like very thin soldiers with unruly brown hair. The crows continued their debate as he ground ink, added water until it was thick and crow black. Quick silent brush strokes recorded dark wing feathers, sharp pointed beaks and fragile-looking legs. Satisfied that the image was a good starting point, he stopped. The watery sketch was left to dry. The next day he returned to the image of the crows. Gathering the tools he needed in his studio, he checked their sharpness, testing them on a spare block of old wood. Content that they were ready, he chose the block he would work with. It was smooth to his touch. Yesterday's image was transferred on to the block. The rhythm of preparation began. When all was ready to his satisfaction, he made the first cut, gouging out wood, digging through the grain, releasing small chips of scented wood. The image of the crows began to appear standing proud above the surrounding wood. The sound of the shavings and chips of wood falling on the bench hardly audible as he worked. The hard solid woodcut finished to his satisfaction, yet to be inked and printed, was in sharp contrast to the watery fluid sketch that had been the beginning of this work. The birds gathered.

MOIRA GARLAND

The liberties granted

In that space you hear kaa   or whisper of slim willows
and in that space might have been sakura, ingredients of a heart,
or in the space a toast of umeshu from the apricot tree
splashing rude pinks, mustardy yellow, insistent red.

Instead he offers so many openings.
In those spaces I once heard
that Watanabe was related to a Hawaiian forest maid
her of the slim-legged three-clawed feet.
In those spaces I see a tsunami of Ainu ghosts
open-mouthed as if in a Munch painting.
In those spaces I touch the possibilities of Paris.
In those spaces I taste a glimpse of
sake from a tiny cup on a low table.
In those spaces I smell the self-assurance of
breathing space.

His pen moves with rhythms of lines that we call trees
where a butterfly balances barely shaded.
The crows have flown away to settle on Asahi-dake
warmed by eruptions of hot steam.

CASSIA STEVENS

In a Flash

Ink on skin.
Permanent memorial to his departed dad,
And to the heritage and lineage of his
Long forgotten ancestors.
Scrolling through Instagram , he follows their work
Waiting for the release of the much anticipated
Watanabe Seitei flash tattoo range.

Which will he choose? And where will it go?
Colourful plumage on his bicep?
Exotic flowers on his ankle?
Brooding huddle of crows on his back?
But then he sees the one.
Grabs his keys, stuffs the saved up earnings into his pocket
And crosses town to their studio

Five long hours later, sore and ears thrumming from the needle buzz
He stands shakily and stares at his reflection.
The bare, drooping branches, delicately etched,
Falling across his pale white chest from collar to sternum.
In his mind's eye the bird has just taken flight,
Leaving a silence, an emptiness, a stillness,
A vacuum that cannot be filled.
It's perfect. Exactly how he imagined it.

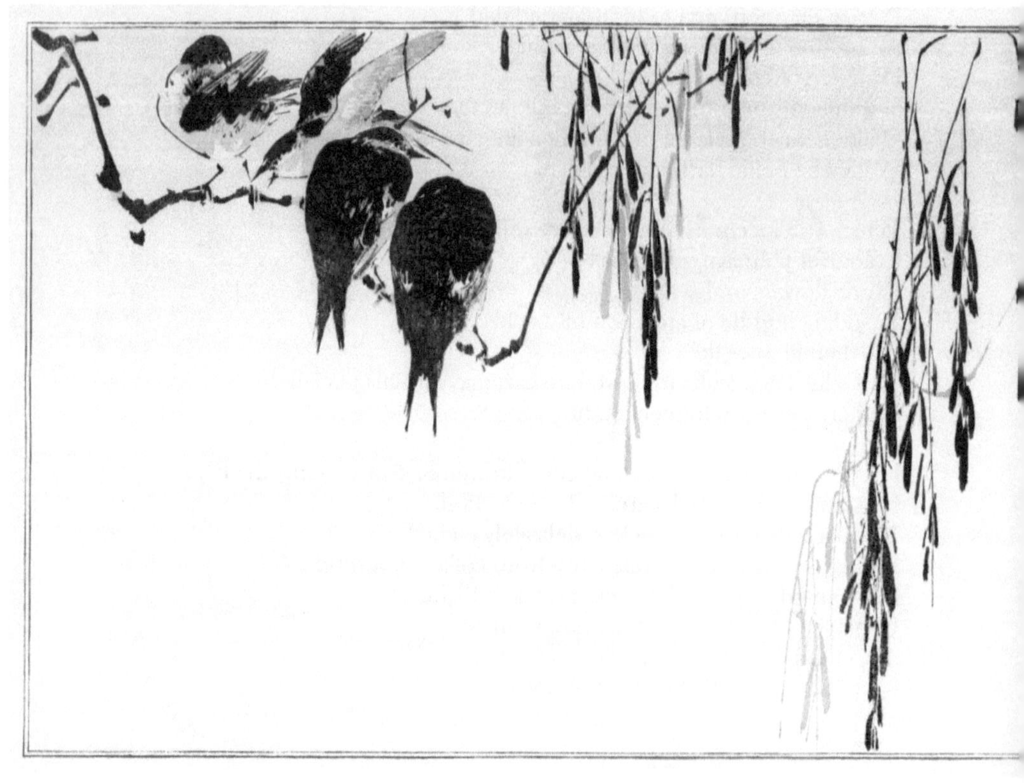

FELICE HARDY

Life

Where does life begin?
Not just with a baby released from the dark
Crying as it bursts into the light

Not just with a puppy, kitten or lamb
Born in a barn, a farm or someone's kitchen
The only offspring or part of a litter or flock

Not just with an egg small and white
From hen, duck, swan or goose
Ready to hatch on the farm or in the grass

Not even an egg we can't identify
From a snake, lizard, croc or turtle
Born in the bush, jungle, sand or sea

But with a seed or bulb
That becomes a bud in springtime
Then bursts into flowers of every colour and size

For these are the signs, the start of life
Some have long lives and some short
From a fluffy chick to a slippery fish

after Christopher James

MICK YATES

when the blackbird sings at dawn

i do not know

what the blackbird sings

for i do not understand

either the lyrics or the tune

it is such a sweet song though

so melodious and full of hope

that any deeper understanding seems irrelevant

he gently serenades me

as i lie in bed in the early morning

he sings i am certain

only about the good things in life

those that lift my spirits

that banish my dark thoughts

he seems content just to be alive

as the passing night slides into a new day